# THORN HILL

Anushka D'Silva

BlueRose
Publishers

First Published in November 2020

**ISBN: 978-93-90432-41-7**

**BLUEROSE PUBLISHERS**
www.bluerosepublishers.com
info@bluerosepublishers.com
+91 8882 898 898

**Cover Design:**
Joshua freitas

**Typographic Design:**
Deepika Matpal

**Distributed by:** BlueRose, Amazon, Flipkart, Shopclues

# ACKNOWLEDGEMENT

**To me,**
For shedding the thorns
And accepting roses

**To you,**
For becoming a part of my journey
And making it yours

**To all,**
For accepting flaws and yourself
And loving them

# THISTLE ROSE

*Rose with petrified thorns*

*Just like my heart*

*A castle full of poisonous darts*

*My mind trapped in this castle*

*As long as it lasts*

*Being close too something so deadly*

*You start to lose sanity*

*While death is nothing but a cause*

*To save yourself from a fall*

# IT'S A HUNT

*Witches of the night*

*Want the humankind to fall apart*

*Nature breathes a sigh*

*As she waits for the day*

*white bright moon*

*But pretty things things fade*

*Rituals and beliefs*

*Beginning of a new turnover leaf*

*Spells and potions*

*A unique vibe*

*Everything's perfect when it's the perfect*

*disguise*

*Be a witch,*

*Run wild*

*There's no point in staying mild*

*You crave my dark soul*
*But I wanna be tamed*
*Wild decisions*
*And a panic room in my head*
*How dark do you have to be to escape?*
*Escape this black hole*
*Pretty eyes can tell stories*
*But mine only show nightmares*
*How long will a dark soul like me take the blame?*

# THIRD VOICE

*She told me she can hear the wolves howling*

*They are getting close*

*She said nothing's gonna change if I act like a*

*rose*

*Waiting for my knight to pick me up*

*She saw lost souls waiting to be found*

*She sees them when whenever I'm around*

*Leftover emotions she threw them away*

*Early morning she begged my happiness to stay*

*She told me she'll fix it*

*My darkness she'll meet*

*Left me alone on the road*

*For strangers to see*

*' Be faithful baby, I'll be here'*

*And now I'm crying in the rain for attention*

*She told me to burn my hopes*

*In the fear of letting go*

*I'm your only one sweetie*

*Don't you know?*

*She tells me she's my only one*
*And then abandons me*
*How long will my soul betray me*
*Giving me false hopes*
*She says I'm just pleaser*
*Holding on to useless hopes*
*Then again she stares at me*
*For losing my senses and crying about it*
*How long will it be before she understands*
*She's the cause and that she is me*

# LITTLE THINGS

*A smile that sparkles her eyes*

*And her presence divine*

*She's what all pretty things are*

*And so is her worth*

*Trouble is what she seeks for*

*But her mind is holy*

*And deep in her mind rests her truly*

*She keeps running from pain*

*It's all about give and take*

*Hopes not getting her anywhere*

*It's useless to pray I swear*

*Her efforts will be counted if she tries*

*She won't be famous unless she dies*

*As a spell caster she'll cast her spell*

*She longs for fame*

*Or lose it all and be a dame*

*The game is hers to play*

*Play safe and live a life of grey*

# WHITE MISERY

*Defend your soul from those who envy you*
*They tell you love is hope*
*And that they don't wanna let you loose*
*They say let go of your past*
*But they don't know that I hid under a mask*
*My mind is too sick to follow rules*
*Or to be tangled up in misery flames*
*These shackles are not too thick*
*How long will they cage me?*
*It will just ruin them*
*I won't look back, cause I'm bound to soar high*

*I'm holding myself in my hands*

*Just like a rose*

*The petals are falling*

*Will my worth be over*

*After they all fall down?*

*Or will I rise as a different rose?*

# LONELINESS ON ITS PEAK

*I'm staring at it*

*The one that pierced through my heart*

*The figure in the mirror looks familiar*

*Closed eyes , reckless decisions*

*The thing fate is in its hands*

*I'm just a tool*

*When I lose value*

*I'll dive in despair*

*Pretty things don't last forever*

*They fade just like actions*

*Play a role*

*Or sit in darkness*

*It's a game anyways*

*So who cares if you win or lose*

# VIOLET

*Grey nights and blue skies*

*Holy days and past desires*

*I'm getting ahead of myself*

*In search of paradise*

*A leap towards peace*

*Would mean I have surrendered*

*But summer's not here yet*

*And I dream too much*

*For if I find my peace*

*I won't lose much*

# DOSE

*Love is like a prison with trust and roses*

*White strings attached to your heart*

*Why do lose control?*

*You keep telling yourself you'll survive*

*Survive what? Love?*

*You said it's fate*

*But you wanna run away*

*A white lie from your mouth is just a lie now*

*You say I'm like rose thorns*

*Sharp like knife and out of your league*

*That I'm not filling up your fantasies*

*But instead eating them*

*You know I'm filling up my void*

*And you don't wanna lose a thing*

*So you act like a victim*

*And demolish love's meaning*

# LADY IN THE WAY

*He told me be attractive*

*He told me to be cold*

*He looked in my eyes and said 'baby I'm yours'*

*He tells me to dress hot*

*I want to run but I'll risk what not*

*He tells me he's my fan , oh he's talking about
the body*

*Staring at other girls and judging them like it's
his hobby*

*He locked me in a cell, it's cold here*

*He says ' go crazy my dear'*

*He watches me fall apart*

*And tells me he loves me as he laughs*

*He wants my purity*

*For him darkness always win*

*Even a little hope makes me hopeless*

*But in the end he's my destiny*

# DOUBTFUL

*I see your smile*

*And it keeps me going*

*But as soon as things fall apart*

*I look for lust*

*It's for my lonely self*

*A world I created for me , myself*

*But I doubt my existence*

*By being strong*

*I wanna let loose*

*But not getting betrayed is all I ask for*

# LOST

It's cold here

And I'm numb where is happiness?

Am I lost?

This path that leads to pretty flowers and

demons

Is quite lonely

Doesn't feel like home

What is home anyway

A lost one doesn't need one

Cause we are children of the lone

# PRETTY THINGS

*Pretty little lies baby*
*Don't fall for them*
*They'll get you pinned down for false hopes*
*If I ever shut up about pretty things*
*Will they come to me?*
*Will they find me for peace?*
*Pursuit of nothingness doesn't seem like a bad*
*idea*
*I'll just focus on darkness for help*
*And if I lose my way*
*I hope my soul finds pretty things in the*
*afterlife*

# ENVY

*I made a deal with it*
*Said I'll walk with the burden*
*But all I wanted was a hand to hold*
*Emotions, they are overflowing*
*Don't ignore them*
*We don't have time to think*
*So don't overthink*
*It's a cage and you're trapped*
*You fell for a lie , how pathetic*
*Your envy will kill you*
*And soon you'll feed on it*
*It's a joke you know?*
*Life itself is full of envy and you can't escape*

# DANCING WITH THE SWORD

*It's midnight and I'm on the edge*

*Everything I do is watched & noted*

*Emotions are clouded*

*I can't feel through*

*Your problems are your decisions they say*

*I tired to look in the mirror for the pathetic me*

*But why do I always blame the society*

*If being in disguise is what you love*

*Then I'm the best sword you'll ever find*

# CHOICE

*2:00 am wrapped in smoke*

*Cause despair's gonna save me from misery*

*Affection is out of the theory*

*But one shot and I'll fall*

*Tell me I can't trust you*

*Tell me humans are cruel*

*But hope is what all want*

*And that will give birth to betrayal soon*

*You want a ride?*

*You'll get one, danger at your door step*

*Babe choose wisely*

# TEARS

*I hope to fall with you*

*We'll ride the misery together*

*It's a headache*

*But I'll swallow my hatred for you*

*It's a risk to even look in your eyes*

*Pain stuck in time*

*Don't you want power?*

*I'll offer it to you*

*Hate is a weapon*

*Make your dreams come true*

*Leave nothing but ashes*

*Useless wishes*

*Efforts are gonna be a waste of time*

*Just jump and my hatred will catch you*

*Don't be scared*

*It's just loneliness*

*Hold my hand and I'll make it disappear*

*Just like your hopes…*

# STRAY

*Abandon one*

*Thrown away*

*She's just leading the path of stray*

*For the ones who aren't welcomed*

*And the ones who lost their worth*

*Tho mending to their needs would just be*

*charity*

*But a fallen one should bare the fate*

*For things like luck don't exist*

*She holds her sword for the valley is deep*

*Fear is a rival*

*Would you let it crush you?*

*Or would you reborn through it?*

*It's just a matter of time*

*Before you embrace that you are falling apart*

*Even tho you are just living*

*Your soul searches for warmth*

*Don't let it stray you more*

# WHITE LADY

I saw a path leading to thorns

White snow on the red blooded bushes

Small walk through it and I got a cut

The thorns were poisoned

The blood gushing down

Hoping to escape

In my sight I see a mirror

Lady in it smiles she tells me I don't have to go

through this

The lady looks familiar

Is that me?

The snow froze and so did time

But the cut still pains

I'm not stuck I'm just hesitating

For going back means failure in life

Is it worth it tho?

What makes it so sure that I won't run away

again

*There's a door in front of me*

*It's huge and stands tall*

*I can't look back now*

*Red, the color of danger*

*Life's never smooth*

*We just gotta sail through they said*

*But my boat sank*

*And I'm watching the sunset from the shore*

*I want the white lady to not give up on me*
*I want her to walk me through this*
*Turn my thorns to roses*
*My dreams to hope*

*We'll be there they said*

*Just look back we'll never leave*

*No human can compare to us*

*We are your hope and your help*

*And just like that my demons became my home*

*There are times I don't understand myself*

*Should I give in?*

*Or should I rebel?*

*Whatever it is,*

*I'll end up with myself again*

*Is it a curse or a blessing?*

*Or just my stupidity?*

# HOME?

*I'm laying in darkness*

*All I see is failure*

*I'm looking for light*

*Where's my destination?*

*I watched my demons lay with me*

*They said their my hope and escape*

*This house knows my desires*

*And I'm a ghost walking in it*

*Will I be free if the house crumbles?*

*Or would it trap me?*

*I'm a double edged sword*

*But the walls whisper me to run away*

*How far will I go till I return back home?*

# A PATH

*Everything seems like a dream now*

*It's funny how I grew*

*The thorns are gone*

*There's a sea in front of me now*

*I wish I knew how to swim*

*I fell in love with the sea*

*I wanna fly with it*

*Embrace it and explore*

*A clear path calling out to me*

*I can see thunder and storms beyond*

*But even if I drown*

*I'll still float*

*For the sea will love me right?*

# EMBRACING

*In this room*

*I see so many people*

*who mask their true selves*

*I'm one of them*

*But if I face you , does that mean I'm true to*

*myself?*

*How deep had I gone?*

*I see sun rays from the deep end*

*I'm sinking*

*But this time I won't fight*

*I'll accept it*

# GOING AFTER STARS

*I'm crying tears of sweetness*

*My dreams are still too far*

*Far, way beyond the sea*

*Is my love for it enough ?*

*Or will it run out?*

*I saw stars in the sea*

*Pretty , glittering*

*I wanna aim higher*

*But if I fall*

*will the sea catch me?*

---

*I'm changing my path?*
*The moon looks so pretty*
*And the sea is so calm*
*I hear the stars sing to the moon*
*Such a sight*
*I'm sitting in the sea*
*It's getting lonelier every night*

# MOONLIGHT

*I thought if I told you about the moon*

*And showed you my scars*

*Then you won't put me behind those judge bars*

*For the moon has phases just like me*

*Sone days have downs*

*And some are pretty sweet*

# GUILTY

*The stars were so quiet to my wish*
*I plead guilty for wanting more*
*I just wanted something real*
*And hope for me*
*But the stars don't want me yet*
*And the sea feels betrayed*
*Now who's gonna catch me?*

# WAR OF STARS

*Let the stars lean on to your touch*

*And the the queen bow down to your embrace*

*Eternity is long enough*

*For the wars in your head*

# BETRAYING MYSELF

*I'm crying to the stars now*

*Be my friend*

*It gets lonely in the sea*

*Tho the sea is very gentle*

*And I'm ready to embrace it*

*But I need more*

*It's beauty captivated me*

*So I called out to the stars*

*And just like that*

*I'm going back to the thorns…*

*I keep dreaming about the garden*

*Not appreciating the sea*

*I told the sea about my dreams*

*He told me those are just glistening illusions*

*I'll embrace them*

*For these illusions will let me see my world*

*The one I'm going after*

*As it has my happiness*

*Love's not a way out*

*But let's try it*

*I feel like I can achieve anything*

*If I fall in love with my self*

*My hunt for trust and love*

*Will be over*

*When I finally accept myself*

*I have been pearls with me*

*The ones I stole from the sea*

*As a parting gift*

*I'm gonna try my love*

*With the roses and thorns again*

# I'M HOME
## ( BACK TO THE THORN GARDEN)

*I'm sitting on a path*

*It's deserted but was once used*

*There are thorns around me*

*But this time it's different*

*The thorns are protecting me*

*I'm crying again*

*Why?*

*This is my home*

*I'm finally home!*

*It keeps flowing*

*I see it slipping through my fingers*

*My body feels lighter than before*

*The thorns in my garden have been replaced*

*with daises*

*There are butterflies everywhere*

*This seems far from a nightmare*

*I see sun rays in my room*

*Am I not trapped anymore?*

*Or is it the calm before the storm?*

# SCARLET

*I'm sitting in garden*

*There are roses everywhere*

*Just like the their color red*

*They are full of mystery and love*

*I sense someone else here*

*He looks so full of hope*

*He's on the other side of the wall*

*I wanna tell him about my dreams*

*But if I shatter the wall*

*Will the storm come in?*

*He says he likes my smile*

*Does he like me enough to break the wall?*

*And if he does break it*

*Will he be my Prince Charming?*

*Prince Charming is just an excuse*

*I just wanna be free*

*But rather than being lonely*

*I'll hang on to the boy who likes my smile*

*A journey together doesn't sound so bad*

*Tho we'll separate one day*

*But it won't be as sad as it was supposed to get*

*For prince are a fairytale*

*And queens are reality*

*The throne belongs to the realest*

*For lies won't take you far*

*But dreams will.*

*I'm climbing down the hill now*

*It had become my home for a while*

*But I can't stay there*

*For even though I have thorns*

*Roses will bloom one day*

*And staying there means my mind will sway*

*I have been running*

*Running, because I'm scared of myself*

*What if I'm the failure*

*That I think I am*

*Can I save myself*

*From my thorns?*

*I had a dream*

*I'm sitting in a rose garden*

*No more shackles*

*No more walls*

*Just me and a mirror*

*There's no lady in it*

*I just see me*

*And I smile at myself*

*As I have been set free*

*Through this journey*
*I found myself*
*Though I'm proud of myself in whatever I do*
*Falling in love with myself*
*Was the best thing I have ever done to myself*

*I look up sun rays drawing in*

*It's the beginning*

*It's the dawn*

*Summers are gonna be sweet*

*Bitter will wash away*

*Tears will hold back*

*Cause happiness is here to stay*

*I keep sinking in your eyes*

*Why do you keeping running away?*

*Let me hold your hand*

*And we can look at the stars*

*No fancy expectations*

*Just you and me*

*Your smile is like sunshine*

*And you crying is a disaster*

*You want the world to accept you*

*I'll be your world girl*

*Even if you fall apart*

*I'll be there for you*

                                 - **To myself**

*I have always been obsessed with roses*

*Tho I'm a sunflower*

*But people crave pretty things right?*

*Tho they hold power*

*Don't let them make you think*

*That you aren't enough*

*All flowers are pretty*

*In their own way*

*And every flower attracts a bee*

**- To my readers**